Family and Friends,

POEMS FOR CHILDREN

By Carolyn Flower

ILLUSTRATIONS BY COLLEEN COMER

Special Thanks To:
Dorothy Strege

Family Car

Our car is a truck;
　　it's high and it's wide.
There's just room for Mom,
　　Dad and me inside.

With Dad at the wheel
　　we go for a ride,
looking down on cars
　　and bikes we pass by.

I bet my friends think
　　I have all the luck.
Mom says, "Get the car!"
　　Dad brings 'round the truck.

A Good Plan

I know I could spell better
if I found the right letter,
but letters get lost in my head.

I see them on every store,
on street signs I see lots more
and they fill up the books I've read.

But, what would really be neat
would be letters I could *eat*–
just a big bunch all in a group.

Then I'd open my mouth wide
and pour all of them inside.
"Mom, can we have alphabet soup?"

Vacation Morn

Dawn had just begun to creep
when Mom woke me from sound sleep,
sent me through grass–wet and deep–
in my stumbling, still-bare feet.

I heard baby birds "cheep, cheep"
and my Dad's car horn "beep, beep."
Mom said, "Not a peep–a peep!–
do I want from that back seat!"

Wishing me to stay asleep
she'd piled blankets in a heap.
But I knew I'd better keep
awake–or miss my chance to eat.

Sleepyhead

Mom calls out, "Time to wake up!"
but I roll over in bed.
Then she opens wide my door,
"Did you hear what I just said?"

A warm, spicy smell floats in
and I sit up really fast.
Are cinnamon rolls baking?
Well, those aren't going to last.

While I'm putting on my clothes,
I hear our neighbor, Miss White.
Yikes! I'd better get out there!
She has a big appetite.

As I step into the hall
my eyes spy old Mister Rand.
He's sitting at our table,
cinnamon roll in each hand.

But the kitchen table's *bare*
except for Mom's coffee cup.
She finds a last roll for me
and says, "Good thing you got up!"

Sweet Dreams

"What's this on my pillow?" Dad called from his room.
"It looks like a whole bunch of flowers in bloom.

And what's that on the end? Could that be pink lace?
Those flowers and frills leave no room for my face!"

"But Dad, I embroidered big roses in red
and sewed on pink lace to give sweet dreams in bed."

"I see," said Dad, "so let's work it out this way:
I'll turn it over at night but up by day . . .

And, thank you, by the way."

Helpful

Chocolate brownie, chocolate ice cream,
chocolate syrup, swirls of whipped cream,
sprinkle of chopped nuts, dark chocolate chips,
all topped with a red cherry.
That was my sister's order.

I say it's too rich, too sweet, too gooey.
She just picks up her spoon and says "phooey."
But she could eat too fast. She could get sick!
It's a little bit scary.
I think I'd better help her.

When I Fell Into Grandma's Mint

When I fell into Grandma's mint
on a sunny summer day,
my feet slipped right off the porch edge
and there in green leaves I lay.

"Help! It smells like giant mint gum!"
What did Grandma have to say?
"Please break off a piece for my tea,
Grandson, since you're out that way."

Fast Food

"You don't want that," my grandpa says,
when I choose a kid-size meal.
"That size is just for little kids.
You can get a better deal."

"Grandpa, I am a little kid,"
I look up at him and say.
"So you are," he says, surprised. "Well,
if that's what you want, okay."

The Artist

"You still make stick people," said my big brother.
"Look! You can't even draw! Just go ask Mother."

Mom said, "Your drawings look real good to me.
I like a picture with a lollipop tree."

So I drew a toothy, green alligator
for her to put on our refrigerator

Grandpa Thinks

My grandpa thinks I ought to know
how corn and other veggies grow.
He says that there is something more
than buying veggies from a store.
He's going to take me for a walk
to show me corn still on the stalk.
But what I really want to see
is where they grow the corn candy.

Time with a Friend

Time to take a walk,
time to have a good talk,
to write on the sidewalk with chalk.

Then time to go home,
so I used my friend's phone
to say I could walk back alone.

Houses weren't the same.
This wasn't how I came.
I was lost and I was to blame.

Then, who did I see?
Papa! He came for me!
I was happy as I could be.

Sleepover

Chinese checkers on the lawn
Monopoly played till dawn
scary stories through the night
eyes propped open till it's light
cold drinks, cookies, apples, too
chips dipped up with lots of goo
pestering from my brother
"Quiet, please!" from my mother
"You kids go to sleep!" from Dad.
What a great party we've had!

At Aunt Margaret's

I like to visit with Great Aunt Margaret
though her apartment is quite small,
and is crammed with newspapers, magazines, books
and old photographs on the wall.

While Mom and Aunt talk and drink tea from thin cups,
they forget that I'm even here.
Till Mom holds a finger to her lips and says,
"Sh-h-h. Little pitchers have big ears."

But wait, I want to hear more about husbands!
Were there really five different men?
The only man I heard of was the last one,
the one that I called Uncle Ken!

When Mom stands to leave and Aunt sets down her tea,
I ask, "Can I take that for you?"
"Of course!" says my aunt, and she gives me a smile.
"What a kind, thoughtful thing to do."

In the kitchen as I set the thin cup down,
Aunt reaches up high on a shelf.
She pulls down a shiny tin box, lifts the lid,
and says to me, "Here, help yourself."

"Thank you," I say–my mind on what I heard–while
unwrapping a chocolate ball.
And I see my aunt in a different light
as I follow Mom down the hall.

Rules for Friends

Laugh at their jokes
smile at their folks
say "sorry" when wrong
in troubles stay strong
be quick with a hug
but slow to feel smug
have fun from the start
but the most important part
keep an open heart.

Surprise

"Daddy, Daddy, where are you going?"
"Well, I'm just seeing friends down the street."
"Will you bring us back ice cream, Daddy?
Please? We need a real cold summer treat."

"Now, you kids don't need any ice cream.
You can eat snacks you've already got."
"But, Daddy, there's nothing really cold
and all day we've been sweaty and hot."

"Drink water with ice cubes," said Daddy,
then got in his truck and drove away.
We sat on the front porch for a while,
trying to think of a game to play.

And then – We could barely believe it! –
Daddy pulled to the curb with no talk.
He leaned over, opened the truck door,
rolled a pint of ice cream up the walk.

"Thank you, Daddy!" he heard us all shout
as he drove off without getting out.

Grandma Says

Grandma says I'm
her sugar lump
her sweet patootie
her pot of jam.
And I am.

Linked

My good friend Della
is also friends with Stella
though Stella's best friend is Amy
who's a friend to Jamie.
Jamie's friend is Eileen
so doesn't it seem–
in the friendship link
which is clear, I think–
that Eileen would be a friend of mine?
And not cut into line?

Ahoy, Matey!

We're sailing on the ocean
along the Spanish Main.
It could be days or even weeks
before we're home again.

We'd like to have you join us,
just bring along a snack
and tell my mom it'll be a while
before I'm coming back.

My Friend's House

Quietly, my friend and I read books.
Whispering, we get all our homework done.
Giggling, we eat snacks while her mom cooks.
Resting, we sit and talk, just one-on-one.

I like the quiet ways at my friend's.
At my own house–as anyone can see–
the loud, noisy racket never ends!
Which is why my friend loves to visit me.

Perfect Evening

First comes the backyard barbecue:
hot dogs, chips, watermelon, too.

Next, a walk to the ice cream store.
I eat two scoops–no room for more.

Then, playing hide-and-seek is good,
running around the neighborhood.

Last, sleeping out in our backyard
with my dog Chandler keeping guard.

Can I do them all in one night?
Well, when it's my birthday, I might!

Next Morning

Whispers and giggles filled the night.
Now morning sun's way too bright.
A sleepover is so much fun!
But you need sleep when they're done.

I'm looking around our back yard
for a spot that's not too hard.
Just somewhere to lay my tired head–
a cool, cozy, hidden bed.

Here's a spot not easily found!
I can nap; no one's around.
Beneath the lilacs and their shade
I'll just drift off. My bed is made.

Rotten Egg

What can you say about a rotten egg?
To Gabe or Joe or Melody or Peg?

Say it's rotten because it wasn't found.
Say to bury it six feet underground.

Say that egg's making a terrible stink!
Say, "Keep it away from my kitchen sink."

Say whatever you want. Go and tell it.
Just make sure that you don't have to smell it!

A Poem About You

You have a great face
with a wonderful smile!
I hope you use it often
not once-in-a-while.

And I like your hair.
It's the perfect color.
You wouldn't look half as good
with any other.

You seem to be strong.
You just ran really fast!
So take good care of yourself.
Make everything last.

A Natural Friend

A bluebird flying high in the sky
wishes to rest and to build her nest.

A squirrel running 'round on the ground
wants his own place–a wide, leafy space.

A young boy facing gloom in his room
runs to his yard but it's cold and hard.

They need a refuge, a place of safety.
What could it be? Why not a tree?

Belonging

Having family
is like having friends call you
to come sit with them.

The End